# Moths

by Mari Schuh

Bullfrog
Books

# Ideas for Parents and Teachers

Bullfrog Books let children practice reading informational text at the earliest reading levels. Repetition, familiar words, and photo labels support early readers.

## Before Reading

- Discuss the cover photo. What does it tell them?

- Look at the picture glossary together. Read and discuss the words.

## Read the Book

- "Walk" through the book and look at the photos. Let the child ask questions. Point out the photo labels.

- Read the book to the child, or have him or her read independently.

## After Reading

- Prompt the child to think more. Ask: Have you ever seen a moth? Where was it flying? How did you know it was a moth?

Dedicated to the Fairmont Area School District—MS

Bullfrog Books are published by Jump!
5357 Penn Avenue South
Minneapolis, MN 55419
www.jumplibrary.com

Library of Congress Cataloging-in-Publication Data

Schuh, Mari C., 1975- author.
 Moths / by Mari Schuh.
    pages cm. -- (Insect world)
  Summary: "This photo-illustrated book for early readers tells about the physical features of moths and briefly describes their life cycle. Includes picture glossary"--Provided by publisher.
  Audience: Ages 5 to 8.
  Audience: K to grade 3.
  Includes bibliographical references and index.
  ISBN 978-1-62031-086-1 (hardcover) --
ISBN 978-1-62496-154-0 (ebook)
  1. Moths--Juvenile literature. I. Title.
 II. Series: Schuh, Mari C., 1975- Insect world.
  QL544.2
  595.78--dc23
                           2013039899

Series Editor: Rebecca Glaser
Series Designer: Ellen Huber
Book Designer: Anna Peterson
Photo Researcher: Kurtis Kinneman

All photos by Shutterstock except: Adrian Davies/naturepl.com, 4; Alamy, 23 ml; iStock, 24; blickwinkel/Alamy, 18; Dreamstime, 23 tl; Jim Almond, 14–15, 23 bl; Kim Taylor/naturepl.com, 5; Meul/ARCO/naturepl.com, 16–17; Robert Thompson/naturepl.com, 9; Stan Malcolm, 6–7, 7 (inset), 23 br; T3rmiit|Dreamstime.com, 17 (inset)

Printed in the United States of America at Corporate Graphics, in North Mankato, Minnesota.
6-2014
10 9 8 7 6 5 4 3 2 1

# Table of Contents

# Moths in the Night

The sky is dark.
Moths fly at night.

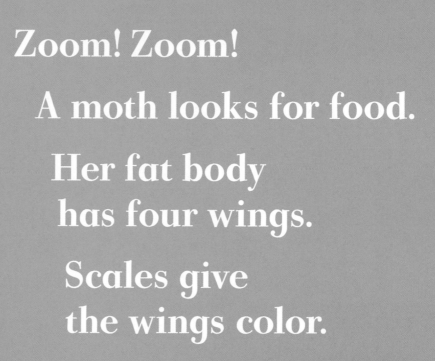

Zoom! Zoom!

A moth looks for food.

Her fat body
has four wings.

Scales give
the wings color.

scales

Oh no!

A crow!

The moth hides
in a tree.

Her dull color helps her hide.

She is safe.

antenna

See her wide antennas?
They look like feathers.
They smell for food.

Here is food.

Sip. Sip.

She sips nectar.

She gives off a scent.

A male moth smells her.

He is miles away.

He flies to her.

They mate.

15

eggs

She lays eggs.

Look!

A caterpillar hatches.

He eats and eats.

He grows.

caterpillar

He makes a cocoon.

Now he is a pupa.

The pupa rests.

cocoon

He turns into a moth.

His wings dry.
Soon he will fly, fly away!

# Parts of a Moth

**tongue**
A moth uses its long tongue to sip nectar from flowers.

**antenna**
A moth uses its antennas to smell and feel. Many moths have thick antennas that look like feathers.

**leg**
A moth has six legs, like all insects.

**wing**
A moth has four wings. Moth wings are often dull colors.

# Picture Glossary

**caterpillar**
A wormlike creature that later changes into a moth.

**nectar**
A sweet liquid found in flowers.

**cocoon**
A silky covering made by moths to keep safe during the pupa stage.

**pupa**
The third stage of a moth's life; pupas change into moths.

**mate**
To join together to make young.

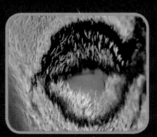

**scales**
Tiny, thin parts that cover a moth's wings and body.

# Index

# To Learn More

Learning more is as easy as 1, 2, 3.

1) Go to www.factsurfer.com

2) Enter "moths" into the search box.

3) Click the "Surf" button to see a list of websites.

With factsurfer.com, finding more information is just a click away.